大堡礁

Sharing the Planet | Non-Fiction Series

Copyright © 2022 by Level Learning, INC. and Washington Yu Ying PCS™
Original and Edited Text Copyright © 2022 by Washington Yu Ying PCS™

All rights reserved. No part of this book in whole or part may be reproduced without written permission from the publisher.

Published by Level Learning, INC.
Content Contributors:
Washington Yu Ying PCS™ - Qianyi (Shirley) Zhang, Pearl Zao He You
Level Learning - Jingyao Qi

Illustrations by: Josh Taira

Leveling classification based on Level Learning standard.
For full description, visit www.levellearning.com

ISBN 978-1-64040-060-3
Simplified Chinese Edition

About Level Learning:
Level Learning provides a literacy focused curriculum specifically designed for K-12 Chinese as a Second Language classrooms. Our program offers 20 levels of specific and detailed objectives, leveled texts and passages, mastery-based online assessment, and analytics to enable data-driven instruction. Level Learning reading curriculum for both literature and informational text emphasize grammar and comprehension skills to help teachers develop confident and independent Chinese language readers. The non-fiction series of books are specifically designed to support our informational text course based on multiple national standards. To learn more about our entire offering, visit www.levellearning.com.

About Washington Yu Ying PCS™:
Washington Yu Ying PCS is a Mandarin English dual language immersion International Baccalaureate (IB) World school. Yu Ying's mission is to inspire and prepare young people to create a better world by challenging them to reach their full potential in a nurturing Chinese/English educational environment. Yu Ying's comprehensive IB, dual immersion curriculum equips students with global competencies for success in the real world. As a leader in immersion education, Yu Ying is determined to advance Chinese language programs and global citizenry education by helping other schools create and strengthen their Chinese programs. For more information, email: products@washingtonyuying.org

大堡礁位于澳大利亚东北部的珊瑚海，是全世界最大的珊瑚礁群。大堡礁包括3000多个珊瑚礁群和几百个小岛。

大堡礁全长2000多公里，是世界七大自然景观之一。甚至在太空，你也可以看到这个伟大的自然景观。

大堡礁是由数十亿条珊瑚虫组成的，是世界上最大的生命结构体。除了美丽的珊瑚岛，在大堡礁中还居住着各种各样的鱼类和珍奇的海洋生物。据统计，仅热带鱼就有1500多个品种。

大堡礁以它的美丽每年吸引着成千上万的游客。人们或乘船,或潜水,近距离地欣赏五颜六色的珊瑚群和丰富多彩的海洋生物。

可是，近年来由于全球变暖，使得海水温度升高。水温升高会引起珊瑚白化，也就是会导致珊瑚死亡。再加上海洋污染越来越严重，大堡礁的生存面临着极大的威胁。

大堡礁国家海洋公园的科学家说，在1998年，只有9%的珊瑚白化。到了2016年，大堡礁的北部已经有三分之二的珊瑚遭到破坏！

这样下去,这片宝贵的珊瑚礁群很快就会从地球上消失。所以,每年都有来自世界各地的志愿者加入保护大堡礁组织。志愿者们帮助渔船远离大堡礁,告诉游客如何保护珊瑚等等。

希望全球变暖和海洋污染等问题可以得到解决，这样大堡礁就会恢复它的美丽了。

Glossary

	Pinyin	English Definition
大堡礁	dà bǎo jiāo	Great Barrier Reef
澳大利亚	ào dà lì yà	Australia
珊瑚	shān hú	coral
海	hǎi	ocean
礁群	jiāo qún	reef system
岛	dǎo	island
公里	gōng lǐ	kilometer
世界七大自然景观	shì jiè qī dà zì rán jǐng guān	Seven Wonders of the World
数	shù	several
十亿	shí yì	billion
珊瑚虫	shān hú chóng	coral polyps
组成	zǔ chéng	make up, constitute
生命	shēng mìng	life
结构体	jié gòu tǐ	structure

	Pinyin	English Definition
珍奇	zhēn qí	rare
仅	jǐn	only
热带	rè dài	tropical
成千上万	chéng qiān shàng wàn	thousands and thousands
游客	yóu kè	tourist
乘船	chéng chuán	to travel by ship
潜水	qián shuǐ	to dive, to go underwater
欣赏	xīn shǎng	to appreciate
五颜六色	wǔ yán liù sè	colorful
丰富多彩	fēng fù duō cǎi	rich and colorful
全球变暖	quán qiú biàn nuǎn	global warming
温度	wēn dù	temperature
升高	shēng gāo	rise
白化	bái huà	bleaching

Glossary

	Pinyin	English Definition
导致	dǎo zhì	to cause, to lead to
污染	wū rǎn	pollution
越来越	yuè lái yuè	more and more
严重	yán zhòng	serious
生存	shēng cún	survival
面临	miàn lín	facing
威胁	wēi xié	threat
破坏	pò huài	damage
消失	xiāo shī	disappear
志愿者	zhì yuàn zhě	volunteer
保护	bǎo hù	to protect
组织	zǔ zhī	organization
解决	jiě jué	to solve
恢复	huī fù	to restore

www.ingramcontent.com/pod-product-compliance
Lightning Source LLC
Chambersburg PA
CBHW041222070526
44584CB00001B/57